MATHA J. RUSSELL

BEYOND ANXIETY

Natural Remedies, Practical Solutions, and Self-Care for Women's Mental Wellness

First edition

This book was professionally typeset on Reedsy.
Find out more at reedsy.com

Contents

Introduction — 1

Chapter One: Navigating the Emotional Landscape — 7

  Common Anxiety Triggers for Women — 7

  Strategies for Managing Anger, Worry, and Fear — 9

  How Past Experiences Can Shape Anxiety — 11

Chapter Two: Building a Supportive Mindset — 13

  Cultivating Positive Self-Talk and Challenging Negative Thoughts — 13

  The Power of Positive Affirmations — 15

  Overcoming Shame and Stigma — 16

Chapter Three: Your Anxiety Management Toolkit — 18

  Mindfulness and Relaxation Techniques — 18

  Cognitive-Behavioral Strategies for Managing Anxiety — 20

  Creative Outlets: How Art Can Ease Anxiety — 22

Chapter Four: Lifestyle Interventions for Anxiety Management — 25

  Nutrition and Exercise — 25

  Sleep Hygiene and its Role in Anxiety Relief — 27

  Nature Therapy and Ecopsychology — 28

Chapter Five: Seeking Professional Help — 31

  Understanding Therapy Options — 31

  Medication: When and How to Consider Pharmaceutical Support — 32

  Exploring Alternative and Complementary Therapies — 34

Chapter Six: Nurturing Relationships — 35

  Building Healthy Boundaries and Assertiveness Skills — 35

  Communication Strategies for Effective Support Networks — 37

  Strategies for Resolving Conflict and Building Stronger Relationships — 38

Chapter Seven: Overcoming Setbacks — 41

Embracing Imperfection: Strategies for Letting Go of
Perfectionism: 41
Learning and Growing from Setbacks   42
Embracing Risk and Uncertainty: Cultivating Resilience   44
Chapter Eight: Empowerment through Self-Care   46
The Importance of Self-Care for Women's Mental Health   46
Creating Personalized Self-Care Plans   48
Radical Self-Love: Embracing Your Authentic Self   49
Conclusion   51

Introduction

Did you know? Anxiety disorders are the most prevalent mental ailment in the United States, affecting more than 40 million persons. Even more strikingly, women are twice as likely as males to feel anxiety during their lives. Perhaps you recognise this: continual stress, social worries, and physical ailments that leave you feeling exhausted. Perhaps someone you care about is facing similar issues.

The good news is that, despite its prevalence, anxiety does not need to define you. This book provides you with effective ways to manage anxiety and develop a calmer, more confident you. Consider exchanging the continual weight of stress for a lightness of spirit. Imagine yourself navigating social settings with ease, not terror. This transformation is within reach. Join me on this journey to restore your inner peace and create a thriving life together.

Understanding Anxiety in Women

Anxiety is a natural human emotion that causes emotions of concern, uneasiness, trepidation, and unease. It's a typical reaction to stressful conditions that keeps us aware and ready to deal with potential threats.

Anxiety disorder is defined as excessive, chronic anxiety that interferes with daily life. This can show in a variety of ways, including physical symptoms such as rapid heartbeat and shortness of breath, as well as intrusive thoughts and avoidance behaviors.

Generalized Anxiety Disorder versus Specific Phobias

There are various types of anxiety disorders, however, the two most frequent for women are:

1. **General Anxiety Disorder (GAD):** People with GAD experience excessive worry and anxiety about a wide range of everyday issues, including finances, health, relationships, and work deadlines. This worry is generally chronic and difficult to manage, causing severe anguish and impairment in daily life.
2. **Specific Phobias:** Specific phobias are acute feelings of fear or anxiety that are caused by a specific object or scenario. Common phobias include a fear of heights, spiders, public speaking (social phobia), and enclosed places (claustrophobia). People who have specific phobias will go to tremendous measures to avoid the phobic object or scenario, which can severely limit their lives.

Prevalence of anxiety in women

Studies regularly reveal that women are more prone than men to suffer from anxiety problems. Here are some stats:

- *According to the Anxiety and Depression Association of America (ADAA), women are twice as likely as males to suffer from an anxiety condition each year.*
- *According to the National Institute of Mental Health (NIMH), 23.7% of women will have an anxiety disorder at some point in their lives, compared to 13.9% of males.*

Several reasons could contribute to the higher frequency in women. This includes:

- **Biological factors:** Hormonal fluctuations during a woman's life cycle (e.g., menstruation, pregnancy, and menopause) might alter brain chemistry and contribute to anxiety.

- **Social pressures:** Women frequently confront cultural expectations around work-life balance, beauty, and caregiving responsibilities, which can lead to chronic stress and anxiety.
- **Genetic predisposition:** Women may be more genetically predisposed to developing anxiety problems.

The Mind-Body Connection

Anxiety not only affects the mind; it can also hurt the body. When you're anxious, your body enters "fight-or-flight" mode, generating stress hormones such as adrenaline and cortisol. This prepares you for immediate danger, but when it occurs regularly as a result of persistent anxiety, it can set off a chain reaction of harmful physical consequences. Here are some common ways that anxiety affects physical health.

- **Sleep Disturbances:** Anxiety can make it difficult to fall and remain asleep. You may have racing thoughts, worry about the future, or feel agitated and unable to relax. This sleep deprivation can exacerbate anxiety symptoms, creating a vicious cycle.
- **Digestive Issues:** The "fight-or-flight" response diverts blood flow away from the digestive system, causing constipation, diarrhea, nausea, and stomach cramps. Anxiety can also worsen pre-existing digestive disorders, such as irritable bowel syndrome.
- **Muscle Tension:** Anxiety frequently appears as muscle tension, particularly in the shoulders, neck, and back. This can cause headaches, soreness, and discomfort.
- **Fatigue and Low Energy:** Chronic anxiety can drain and tire you. The persistent stress response depletes your energy reserves, making it harder to concentrate and execute daily chores.
- **Cardiovascular Problems:** Anxiety can raise heart rate, blood pressure, and the likelihood of heart palpitations. Over time, this can lead to more

significant cardiovascular issues.

- **Weakened Immune System:** Chronic stress impairs your immune system, increasing your susceptibility to colds, flu, and other diseases.
- **Sexual Dysfunction:** Anxiety can impair both men's and women's sexual health. It can lower libido, make it difficult to achieve orgasm, and cause erectile dysfunction in men.

Strategies for Addressing Physical Symptoms

When anxiety strikes, your body and mind may feel like they are on overdrive. Fortunately, there are simple but effective relaxation techniques that can help you quiet your nervous system and restore your body's balance. Here are two powerful approaches you can implement in your daily routine:

1. Deep Breathing: This basic relaxation technique is simple to learn and apply anywhere. It slows your heart rate, lowers blood pressure, and activates your body's relaxation reaction.

This is how you do it:

1. **Find a comfortable position:** Sit or lie down in a quiet, comfortable space. Close your eyes if that feels relaxing for you.
2. **Focus on your breath:** Take a slow, deep breath in through your nose for a count of four. Feel your belly expand as you inhale.
3. **Hold your breath briefly:** Hold your breath for a count of two at the top of your inhale.
4. **Exhale slowly:** Slowly exhale through your mouth for a count of six, feeling your belly contract as you release the air.
5. **Repeat:** Repeat steps 1-4 for several minutes, focusing on the sensation of your breath moving in and out of your body.

Tips:

- **Find Your Rhythm:** Experiment with different inhalation and exhalation periods to discover a rhythm that feels natural and relaxing to you.
- **Visualise relaxation:** As you exhale, envision releasing tension through your breath. You can imagine stress melting away or a relaxing image, such as a serene ocean wave.
- **Practice regularly:** Deep breathing techniques will become more effective at reducing anxiety symptoms as you practise them more frequently.

2. Progressive Muscle Relaxation (PMR): This technique involves tensing and relaxing certain muscle groups across the body. By purposefully tensing and releasing muscles, you can become more aware of the physical tension that comes with anxiety and learn to let it go.

This is how you do it:

1. **Find a comfortable position:** Similar to deep breathing, find a comfortable position, sitting or lying down.
2. **Start with your toes:** Begin by tensing the muscles in your toes. Curl your toes tightly towards you and hold for a count of five. Then, completely relax your toes and feel the tension release.
3. **Work your way up:** Continue tensing and relaxing muscle groups progressively up your body. Target major muscle groups in your legs, buttocks, stomach, chest, shoulders, arms, face, and neck.
4. **Focus on the sensation:** As you tense each muscle group, pay attention to the feeling of tension. Then, as you relax, focus on the feeling of release and relaxation spreading throughout your body.
5. **Repeat the cycle:** Complete one full cycle of tensing and relaxing all muscle groups. You can repeat this cycle two or three times.

Tips:

- **Breathe deeply:** Combine PMR with deep breathing for an even stronger effect. Inhale as you tense, then exhale as you relax.

- **Focus on the present moment:** During the exercise, try to concentrate on the physical sensations in your body rather than lingering on your problems or anxiety.
- **Practice regularly:** Like deep breathing, PMR improves with frequent practice.

Chapter One: Navigating the Emotional Landscape

Common Anxiety Triggers for Women

Women encounter specific demands and problems that can lead to anxiety. Here are some frequent triggers you should be aware of:

Work/Life Balance:

- **Juggling responsibilities:** Balancing work commitments, family caring, and household tasks can be daunting, resulting in chronic stress and anxiety.
- **Perfectionism:** The pressure to succeed in all areas can be especially distressing for women. Anxiety can be caused by the dread of failing or falling short of high expectations.
- **Workplace challenges:** Workplace obstacles, such as discrimination, harassment, or a lack of support, can all add to anxiety levels.

Relationships:

- **Relationship conflict:** Disagreements with partners, friends, or family members can cause significant distress.
- **dread of abandonment:** The dread of being alone or losing someone

you care about can cause anxiety, especially in situations of relationship uncertainty.

- **Communication difficulties:** Difficulties communicating demands and creating limits can cause dissatisfaction and anxiety in partnerships.

Social situations:

- **Social anxiety:** Some women find public speaking, meeting new people, and attending large gatherings extremely stressful.
- **dread of judgment:** The dread of being judged or criticized by others can hurt self-esteem and lead to social anxiety.
- **Body image issues:** Societal demands on body image can cause anxiety and a continual sense of self-reflection in social circumstances.

Life Transitions:

- **Major life changes:** Major life changes, such as moving, starting a new career, getting married, or having children, can be exhilarating but also cause anxiety due to uncertainty and problems.
- **Pregnancy and postpartum:** Hormonal variations, as well as the physical and mental strains of pregnancy and postpartum, can cause severe anxiety for some women.
- **Menopause:** Menopause can cause physical and emotional changes that might lead to anxiety symptoms in some people.

Financial Concerns:

- **Financial insecurity:** Concerns about debt, job stability, and making ends meet can be significant sources of chronic stress and anxiety.
- **Financial responsibility:** Women frequently bear the task of managing home money, which can exacerbate the stress and anxiety connected with financial security.

Health Concerns:

- **Chronic health conditions:** Living with a chronic health condition can be physically and emotionally exhausting, exacerbating anxiety symptoms.
- **Health anxiety:** Some women have health-related anxiety, which causes them to worry excessively about prospective ailments and see the doctor frequently.
- **dread of illness:** The dread of getting sick or having a major illness can cause anxiety, especially during pandemics or outbreaks.

Strategies for Managing Anger, Worry, and Fear

Anger, worry, and fear are all powerful emotions that can control our thoughts and behaviours. While these feelings are useful, when they become excessive or overwhelming, they can have a substantial influence on our daily lives. Here are some ways to help you deal with anger, stress, and fear:

1. Journaling to express emotions:

- **Expressing emotions:** Journaling allows you to vent your anger, stress, and fear without judgment. Write down what is bothering you, how it makes you feel, and any bodily sensations that go along with these emotions.
- **Identifying triggers:** Identifying Triggers As you journal over time, you may see patterns and repeating themes that elicit these emotions. Self-awareness can be an effective strategy for managing them.
- **Cognitive reframing:** Use journaling to confront negative thoughts about your feelings. For example, if you're furious, replace the idea "I'm a failure" with something more balanced, such as "This situation is frustrating, but I can learn from it and move on."

2. Mindfulness exercises:

- **Anchoring yourself in the present:** Mindfulness practices can help you become more aware of your emotions in the moment and avoid being swept away by them. To bring your attention back to the present now, focus on your breath, physiological sensations, or surrounding sounds.
- **Detach from negative thoughts:** When worries or fears come, recognize them without passing judgment and gently redirect your focus back to your breath or another anchor in the present.
- **Mindful breathing techniques:** Deep breathing exercises, such as those stated previously, can be especially effective in calming the nervous system and decreasing emotional intensity.

3. Relaxation techniques:

- **Progressive muscle relaxation:** As previously noted, PMR reduces physical tension linked with anxiety and can also be used to manage anger, worry, and fear.
- **Guided Imagery:** Visualisation techniques can take you to a quiet and pleasant environment, encouraging relaxation and decreasing emotional reactivity.
- **Yoga and Gentle Stretching:** Yoga and gentle stretching can help relieve stress and promote relaxation. Yoga mixes movement and mindfulness, making it an effective tool for managing emotions.

4. Communication skills:

- **Assertive Communication:** Express your demands and feelings assertively, without being angry or aggressive.
- **Setting boundaries:** Learn to set appropriate boundaries with people to avoid situations that make you angry, worried, or afraid.
- **Active listening:** Use active listening skills to improve communication with loved ones and prevent misconceptions that can lead to irritation and wrath.

5. Cognitive-behavioral therapy (CBT):

- **CBT** helps identify and confront negative thought patterns that cause emotional suffering. A therapist can help you build better coping skills for dealing with anger, worry, and fear.
- **CBT** is especially useful in recognizing cognitive distortions that fuel these emotions, such as catastrophizing (assuming the worst-case situation) and overgeneralization (drawing broad negative inferences from a single occurrence).

How Past Experiences Can Shape Anxiety

Anxiety might not necessarily result from current pressures. It can sometimes be traced back to earlier experiences that have left a lasting impression. Here's how.

- **Unresolved Trauma:** terrible occurrences such as abuse, neglect, accidents, or witnessing a terrible incident can have long-lasting emotional consequences. If these events are not properly addressed, they might lead to chronic anxiety throughout adulthood.
- **Negative Conditioning:** Early experiences can influence how we see the world and ourselves. If you have previously experienced criticism, judgment, or rejection, you may be more susceptible to concern, fear of failure, or social anxiety.
- **Imprint of Fear:** Fearful encounters might lead to a perception of the world as hazardous or unpredictable. This can result in hypervigilance (being always on alert) and generalized anxiety.

It is important to recognize that not everyone who has had a bad past experiences anxiety. However, if you feel that a previous incident is contributing to current anxiety, do not hesitate to seek expert help.

Here's why getting expert help can be useful:

- **Exploring the root cause:** A therapist can assist you in exploring your past experiences and how they relate to your current anxiety symptoms.
- **Processing Trauma:** Therapy can provide a secure environment in which to process previous trauma and develop healthy coping strategies.
- **Healing and Moving Forward:** By addressing the source of your worry, you may break free and create a more satisfying future.

Chapter Two: Building a Supportive Mindset

Cultivating Positive Self-Talk and Challenging Negative Thoughts

The voice in your head can be your best supporter or your fiercest critic. When worry arises, it frequently intensifies negative thoughts, making you feel worse. But there's good news: you can reinterpret that voice and build a more positive internal conversation.

The Benefits of Positive Self-Talk

Positive self-talk does not imply disregarding obstacles or pretending everything is wonderful. It is about replacing negative self-criticism with positive and helpful words. This change in vocabulary can have a significant impact on your mental state and overall well-being. Here are a few benefits:

- **Increases confidence and self-esteem:** When you convince yourself you can accomplish it, you're more likely to believe it and follow through.
- **Reduces tension and anxiety:** Positive self-talk allows you to approach difficult situations with a calmer and more hopeful mindset.
- **Increases resilience.** Positive self-talk helps you recover from failures and move forward.

Challenging Negative Thought Patterns

Our brains are hardwired for negativity to some extent. It is a survival feature passed down from our ancestors. However, unresolved negative ideas can become like worn trails in your mind, bringing you down a spiral of dread. Here's how you can challenge them.

- **Identify negative thoughts:** The first stage is to become conscious of your cognitive habits. Pay attention to the self-critical messages that arise in your mind when you're anxious.
- **Question the validity:** Don't take negativity as truth. Ask yourself, "Is this thought helpful or accurate?" "Is there another way to look at this situation?"
- **Challenge and reframing:** Once you've detected negative thinking, question its veracity and replace it with a more optimistic and realistic statement. Instead of thinking, "I'm going to mess this up," reframe it as "I'm prepared and I'll do my best."

Here are some strategies for encouraging good self-talk and challenging negative thoughts:

- **Affirmations:** Repeating positive phrases about yourself will help you overcome negative thoughts and enhance your self-confidence. Examples include "I am capable," "I am worthy," and "I am deserving of love and happiness."
- **Visualization:** Imagine yourself excelling in a circumstance that usually causes worry. Concentrate on the sensations of confidence and accomplishment.
- **Gratitude journaling:** Take time each day to reflect on what you are grateful for. This exercise might help you focus on the positive parts of your life and develop a more optimistic view.

The Power of Positive Affirmations

Positive affirmations, whether silent or vocal, can have a powerful impact on your ideas and behaviors. They operate as seeds placed in your mind, and with constant repetition, they can grow into a more self-assured and happy outlook. This is how affirmations work:

Shifting your inner dialogue:

Our inner conversation can be a constant source of self-doubt and pessimism. Affirmations provide a means to break this cycle and replace negative ideas with uplifting messages. By purposefully repeating positive statements, you can begin to confront and rewrite the negative scripts going through your mind.

Neuroplasticity and The Power of Repetition:

The brain is a plastic organ, which means it may develop and adapt throughout our lives. When you repeatedly say affirmations, you build new neural pathways in your brain that encourage positive self-belief. Over time, these positive affirmations become more accessible in your mind, replacing negative thoughts with confidence and optimism.

Boosting Self-Esteem and Self-Efficacy:

Positive affirmations can boost self-esteem and self-efficacy, acting as a motivational tool. Repeating phrases that highlight your skills and capabilities over time might help you improve self-esteem and self-efficacy. This improved confidence can inspire you to take on new challenges and pursue your objectives with greater dedication.

Examples of Confident and Positive Affirmations:

- **"I am capable and confident."**

- **"I am worthy of love and happiness."**
- **"I am strong and resilient."**
- **"I trust my intuition and inner wisdom." "I am learning and growing every day."**
- **"I am surrounded by love and support."**

Tips for Effective Affirmation Practices

- **Personalize your affirmations:** Choose affirmations that relate to you and your personal goals.
- **Present tense with positive phrasing:** Concentrate on the present time and utilize positive language. For example, instead of expressing "I will be confident," state "I am confident."
- **Belief and Feeling:** Repeat affirmations with conviction, attempting to feel the feelings associated with the positive statement. Visualization can help with this process.
- **Consistency is key:** The more often you say affirmations, the more potent their impact will be. Aim to practice every day, even if it is only for a few minutes.

Overcoming Shame and Stigma

Let's Talk About Anxiety: It's Okay to Feel Bad. We've all felt it from time to time: that knot in your stomach before a big presentation, racing thoughts before a date, or concern swirling around an impending deadline. It's a typical human emotion, and you're not alone.

Millions of individuals throughout the world suffer from anxiety problems. It can be a crippling ailment, but there is relief available. What's the first step? Talking about it.

Let us break the stigma:

- **Mental health is equally vital as physical health:** Talking about anxiety should not be considered taboo, just as you would not hesitate to discuss a physical issue.
- **Sharing your challenges can be liberating:** Speaking with a friend, family member, or therapist, or even joining a support group can bring essential insight and connection.
- **Open communication causes a cascade effect:** When we freely discuss anxiety, we normalize it and urge people to seek help if necessary.

Here are some ways to begin the conversation.

- **Share your personal experiences.** Let folks know that you have anxiousness on occasion. Hearing someone else's story can be a very effective approach to connecting.
- **Ask inquiries with sensitivity.** Show genuine concern for how someone else is experiencing.
- **Listen without passing judgment.** Allow others to share their experiences without feeling judged or disregarded.
- **Educate yourselves and others.** Learn about anxiety disorders and share information with others who may be interested.
- **Remember that you are not defined by your anxiety.** It is a part of you, but it does not have to dominate you. You may control your anxiety and live a full life by communicating openly and getting support.

Here are some resources to help:

- **National Institute of Mental Health:** [Anxiety Disorders National Institute of Mental Health (.gov) nimh.nih.gov]
- **Anxiety and Depression Association of America:** [American Association for Depression and Anxiety adaa.org]
- **National Alliance on Mental Illness (NAMI):** [nami national alliance on mental illness nami.org]

Chapter Three: Your Anxiety Management Toolkit

Mindfulness and Relaxation Techniques

Do you feel overwhelmed by anxiety? Take a minute to reflect and reconnect with yourself. Here's a guided experience that uses mindfulness meditation, deep breathing techniques, and progressive muscle relaxation to enhance relaxation and reduce anxiety.

Preparation:

1. **Find a comfortable position:** Sit or lie down in a peaceful, comfortable area where you will not be interrupted.
2. **Closing your eyes is optional:** If it's comfortable, gently close your eyes. If not, relax your eyes and concentrate on a place a few feet in front of you.
3. **Set your intention (optional):** Briefly state your intention for your practice. You may silently tell yourself, "I will allow myself to relax and release tension."

Mindfulness Meditation (5 minute):

1. **Focus on your breathing:** Observe your normal breathing, noticing the

rise and fall of your chest or abdomen with each inhale and exhale. Do not try to regulate your breathing; instead, simply notice it.

2. **Wandering thoughts:** Your mind will naturally wander. When you find yourself buried in thinking, gently return your focus to your breathing without judgment.

3. **Body sensations:** Pay close attention to any physical sensations in your body, without judgment. Look for any areas of tension, tightness, or discomfort.

Deep Breathing Exercises (5 min):

1. **Box Breathing:** Visualise a square box in your head. Inhale slowly through your nose for a count of four, feeling your stomach expand. Hold your breath for a count of four. Exhale slowly through your lips for four counts, feeling your stomach collapse. Hold for four counts, then repeat. Continue for a few minutes.

2. **Diaphragmatic Breathing:** Put one hand on your chest and the other on your stomach. As you inhale, feel your abdomen (not your chest) expand for four counts. Hold for four counts, then gently exhale through pursed lips, allowing your belly to contract for six counts. Repeat for a few minutes.

Progressive Muscle Relaxation (10 Minutes)

- **Start with your toes:** Curl your toes tightly towards you for a count of five, feeling the tightness in your feet. Then, fully relax your toes and feel the tension release (count to five).

- **Move up the body:** Tense and relax muscle groups gradually up your body. Focus on the main muscle groups in your legs, buttocks, stomach, chest, shoulders, arms, face, and neck.

- **Concentrate on the sensation:** Pay attention to how your muscles feel as you tense them. Then, as you rest, concentrate on the sensations of release and relaxation that flow throughout your body.

- **Take a final breath:** After you've performed all of the muscle groups, inhale deeply and exhale slowly, releasing any lingering tension.

Bringing Yourself Back:

- **Wiggle your fingers and toes:** Gently wriggle your fingers and toes to return your attention to the present moment.
- **Take a break:** Take a few moments to sit or lie quietly, enjoying the feeling of relaxation.
- **Open your eyes (optional):** If you have closed your eyes, softly open them and gaze around you.

Remember:

- **Remember to be patient with yourself.** It takes practice to master these strategies.
- **Consistency is essential.** For the best results, perform these exercises regularly.
- **Find out what works for you.** Experiment with different relaxation techniques to see what works best for you.

This guided practice is simply a starting point. There are numerous varieties and tools available online and via mindfulness applications. Discover what speaks to you and build a personalized relaxation practice that promotes your well-being.

Cognitive-Behavioral Strategies for Managing Anxiety

Cognitive Behavioural Therapy (CBT) is a type of therapy that examines the relationship between our thoughts, emotions, and behaviours. CBT's primary principle is to identify and challenge negative thought patterns that contribute to emotional distress, notably anxiety and depression. Here's a breakdown of the process:

1. Identifying Negative Thoughts (Automatic Negative Thoughts, or ANTs):
Our brains are hardwired to be attentive to potential hazards. This might result in a steady stream of ideas, many of which are automatic and occur without our conscious awareness. These habitual beliefs are frequently negative, and cognitive behavioral therapy assists us in recognizing these unhelpful habits.

Here are some instances of unpleasant thoughts relating to anxiety:

- **Overgeneralization:** "I messed up this presentation, so I'm always going to fail."
- **Catastrophising:** "If I don't get this job, I'll never be successful."
- **Mind-reading:** "Everyone thinks I'm a fraud."
- **Disqualifying the Positive:** "They only complimented my work out of pity."

2. confront Negative Thoughts:
CBT can help identify and confront negative thought patterns, leading to more balanced perspectives. Here's how.

- **Question the evidence:** Ask yourself, "Is this thought truly accurate?" Is there evidence to back it up, or is it based on fear or previous experiences?
- **Consider alternative explanations:** Are there any alternative ways to analyze the situation? Instead of thinking, "Everyone thinks I'm a fraud," you could respond, "Maybe they noticed I was nervous, but I did a good job overall."
- **Focus on the facts:** Instead of imagining the worst-case scenario, focus on facts and reality.
- **Develop More Realistic thinking:** Replace negative thinking with more realistic and useful statements. For example, "I made a mistake, but I can learn from it and do better next time."

3. Reframing:

Challenging negative views and replacing them with balanced viewpoints might help reframe your thinking. This alteration might have a big impact on your emotional state. For example, instead of being overwhelmed by fear, you may be encouraged to learn and grow.

CBT Techniques:

- **Journaling:** Writing down your thoughts and feelings might help you recognize trends and combat pessimism.
- **Socratic questioning:** A therapist can help you challenge your negative views and reach more balanced conclusions.
- **Behavioral experiments:** Testing the validity of your negative thoughts with real-world events might be an effective approach to confront them.

Creative Outlets: How Art Can Ease Anxiety

The world might feel overwhelming at times, and worry can have a negative impact on our emotional health. But did you know that artistic expression can be an effective method for reducing anxiety and increasing relaxation? Here's how.

- **Emotional Release:** Creative activities offer a healthy avenue for expressing and processing emotions. Whether you paint your frustrations, write about your problems, or dance your anxiety away, creative expression allows you to safely and productively release pent-up emotions.
- **Mindfulness and Focus:** The act of making art necessitates focus and concentration in the current time. This focus can serve as a mindfulness practice by diverting your attention away from nervous thoughts and worries. As you become immersed in the creative process, ruminating fades, promoting a sense of serenity and harmony.

- **Building Confidence and Self-Esteem:** Creating something you're proud of, regardless of your ability level, can enhance your confidence and self-worth. This sense of success can counteract emotions of inadequacy or self-doubt, which frequently contribute to worry.
- **Problem-Solving and Self-Discovery:** The creative process might involve problem-solving. As you explore different techniques and materials, you may discover unexpected answers or new views that may be applied to other aspects of your life, such as helping you manage anxiety in novel ways. Art may also be a voyage of self-discovery, allowing you to connect with your inner self and express feelings that may be difficult to articulate.

The Beauty of Creative Expression

The beauty of creative expression is its accessibility and universality. There are no rules, no correct or incorrect way to construct. Here are some creative ways to explore:

- **Visual arts:** Explore any visual medium that calls to you, including painting, drawing, sculpture, and collage.
- **Music:** Play an instrument, sing, or simply experiment with making sounds electronically.
- **Writing:** Journaling, poetry, and creative fiction allow you to express yourself through the written word.
- **Movement:** Dance, yoga, or any other type of movement that allows you to connect with your body.

Remember that the emphasis is not on producing a masterpiece, but on the process of creation itself. Let go of perfectionist tendencies and enjoy the delight of inquiry.

Here are some more tips:

- **Begin small:** Do not feel pushed to make grandiose projects. Begin with brief periods of creativity, such as 15 minutes of doodling or coloring.

- **Discover a creative community:** Join an art class, writing group, or online forum to meet individuals who share your enthusiasm for creativity.
- **Make it fun!** The most essential thing is to enjoy the experience and have fun expressing yourself.

Chapter Four: Lifestyle Interventions for Anxiety Management

Nutrition and Exercise

Are you feeling anxious? Don't underestimate the impact of your diet and physical activity. Diet and exercise are critical in reducing anxiety symptoms and improving general well-being. Here's how.

Diet and anxiety:

- **The gut-brain connection:** Our gut microbiome, which consists of trillions of bacteria in our digestive tract, has a huge impact on our mental health. An imbalance in gut bacteria may contribute to anxiety and other mood problems.
- **Nutrient Deficiencies:** Certain vitamins and minerals, such as B vitamins, magnesium, and zinc, can cause anxiety symptoms.
- **Blood Sugar Regulation:** Consuming a well-balanced diet that maintains stable blood sugar levels will help reduce mood swings and irritation, which can exacerbate anxiety.

Here's what you should include in your anxiety-reducing diet:

- **Fruits and veggies:** High in antioxidants and important nutrients, fruits and vegetables promote a healthy gut microbiome and overall well-being.

- **Whole Grains:** Whole grains provide continuous energy and help manage blood sugar levels, which contributes to a more relaxed mood.
- **Lean Protein:** Protein helps control mood-enhancing neurotransmitters such as serotonin and dopamine. Choose lean proteins such as fish, chicken, beans, and lentils.
- **Healthy Fats:** Fats contained in fatty fish, avocados, nuts, and seeds promote brain function and can help lower inflammation, which has been related to anxiety.

Foods to Limit:

- **Processed Foods:** Processed foods are frequently heavy in sugar, harmful fats, and processed carbs, which can lead to blood sugar fluctuations and exacerbate anxiety symptoms.
- **Caffeine and alcohol:** While these substances may have a momentary relaxing effect, they can eventually aggravate anxiety.
- **Sugar:** Sugar crashes can cause heightened anxiety and irritability. Limit your consumption of sugary beverages, processed foods, and refined carbohydrates.

Exercise and Anxiety:

- **Stress Relief:** Exercise is a natural stress reliever. Physical activity causes the release of endorphins, which are brain chemicals that improve mood and relieve pain.
- **Improved Sleep:** Regular exercise can improve sleep quality, and getting enough sleep is essential for managing anxiety.
- **Increased Confidence:** Regular physical activity can improve your mood and self-confidence, making you feel more prepared to handle anxiety-inducing events.

Here are some exercise strategies for reducing anxiety:

- **Find an activity that you enjoy:** If you enjoy your fitness program, you are more likely to stick to it. Consider activities such as walking, running, swimming, dance, yoga, or team sports.
- **Start slowly and gradually Increase Intensity:** Do not attempt to do too much too quickly. Begin with a moderate regimen, then progressively increase the duration and intensity as your fitness progresses.
- **Aim for at least 30 minutes of moderate-intensity exercise on most days of the week.**

Sleep Hygiene and its Role in Anxiety Relief

A good night's sleep is critical to both physical and mental well-being. Sleep deprivation makes us more prone to stress, anxiety, and even sickness. The good news is that you can adopt healthy sleep habits that will help you sleep better and wake up feeling refreshed. Here are a few tips:

Set the Stage for Sleep:

- **Develop a steady sleep schedule:** Every day, even on weekends, go to bed and get up at the same hour. This helps to maintain your body's normal sleep-wake cycle (circadian rhythm).
- **Create a calm nighttime routine:** Relax for 30-60 minutes before bedtime with soothing activities such as reading, taking a warm bath, or mild stretching. Avoid screens with bright light emissions (phones, computers, and televisions) for at least an hour before bedtime because the blue light emitted can interfere with sleep.
- **Optimize your sleeping environment:** Make sure your bedroom is dark, quiet, cool, and clear of clutter. Invest in blackout curtains, earplugs, a comfortable mattress, and pillows.

Habits to avoid:

- **Limit caffeine and alcohol:** Caffeine may provide a momentary lift, but it might impair sleep later in the night. Avoid coffee in the afternoons and evenings. Alcohol may help you fall asleep faster, but it impairs your sleep quality throughout the night.
- **Avoid large meals and sugary snacks before bedtime:** A light, healthy snack before bedtime is acceptable, but avoid large meals or sugary snacks, which can affect digestion and sleep.
- **Get regular exercise:** Regular physical activity improves sleep, but avoid severe exercise close to bedtime because it might be stimulating.

Listen to your body:

- **Relaxation Techniques:** If you're having difficulties falling asleep, try relaxing techniques like deep breathing or progressive muscle relaxation.
- **Light exposure:** Get some natural sunshine exposure throughout the day, particularly in the morning. This helps to control your circadian rhythm.
- **Do not force sleep:** If you can't fall asleep after 20 minutes, get out of bed and do something quiet until you're weary. Do not lie awake in bed for extended periods, as this can cause sleep anxiety.

Nature Therapy and Ecopsychology

In today's fast-paced society, many people seem to live with anxiety all the time. But did you know that the natural world contains a potent remedy for this persistent feeling? Spending time in nature has been found to provide a wide range of benefits for anxiety control, relaxation, and general well-being. Here's how.

Nature as a stress buster:

- **Reduces stress hormones:** Studies have shown that merely being in nature, whether for a walk in the park or a walk in the woods, can reduce cortisol levels, the body's principal stress hormone. This decrease in stress hormones leads to a more relaxed bodily and mental state, making worry feel less overwhelming.

- **Attention Restoration Theory:** Our brains are continually inundated with stimuli in the digital world. Nature offers a respite from this constant onslaught. Nature's sights, sounds, and smells have a soothing influence on our attention, allowing us to relax and defocus from our troubles. This mental break can effectively alleviate anxious symptoms.

Improving Mood and Wellbeing:

- **Increased Happiness:** Spending time outside exposes you to more natural sunlight, which boosts the production of vitamin D and serotonin, both of which help regulate mood. Basking in the sun can make you feel happier and more hopeful, counteracting the negative emotions connected with anxiety.
- **Connection to Something Bigger:** Immersion in nature might help you feel more connected to something greater than yourself. This connection can be calming and provide a sense of perspective, making your worries appear less significant.

The Power of Nature's Sensory Experience:

- **Mindfulness in Nature:** The natural environment is full of sights, sounds, smells, and textures that can captivate our attention in the present moment. Focusing on the sound of birds singing, the sensation of soft grass beneath your feet, or the beautiful patterns on a leaf can all help you achieve a state of awareness and divert you from anxious thoughts and worries.
- **Physical Activities in Nature:** Spending time outside with physical activity can have a double effect on anxiety control. Going for a walk, hike, or bike ride in nature not only promotes physical activity, but it also provides

stress-relieving and mood-boosting effects.

Nature For Everyone:

The beauty of nature's anxiety-relieving properties is that they are available to anybody. You don't have to embark on a week-long camping excursion to gain the rewards. Even modest amounts of nature can make an impact. Here are a few ideas:

- **Take a walk through a nearby park or greenspace.**
- **Sit on a bench and take in the sights and noises around you.**
- **Have lunch outside.**
- **Practice mindfulness exercises in nature.**
- **Garden or care for houseplants.**

Chapter Five: Seeking Professional Help

Understanding Therapy Options

Here is a brief overview of three common therapies for anxiety and other mental health conditions:

Cognitive behavior therapy (CBT):

- *Focuses on identifying and confronting negative thought patterns that cause emotional pain.*
- *Teaches how to recognize and reframe problematic thinking.*
- *Create coping mechanisms for handling anxiety-provoking circumstances.*
- *Change the behaviors that cause anxiety.*
- *Journaling, cognitive restructuring, and exposure therapy are all frequently used strategies.*

Dialectical Behavior Therapy (DBT):

- *Dialectical Behaviour Therapy (DBT) is a type of cognitive-behavioral therapy that addresses emotional dysregulation and borderline personality disorder.*

Teaches skills in four key areas:

- **Mindfulness:** Mindfulness entails remaining present in the moment and noticing emotions without judgment.
- **Distress Tolerance:** Healthily managing tough emotions.
- **Interpersonal Effectiveness:** Interpersonal effectiveness entails communicating effectively and developing healthy connections.
- **Emotional Regulation:** Emotional regulation is the process of identifying and efficiently managing emotions.

Acceptance and Commitment Therapy (ACT):

- *Acceptance and Commitment Therapy (ACT) is a newer technique that relies on CBT ideas while emphasizing acceptance of challenging thoughts and feelings.*

Focuses on:

- *Accepting that certain ideas and feelings are beyond our control.*
- *Identifying your basic principles and what matters to you in life.*
- *Taking deliberate action to live a meaningful life by your ideals, even in the face of anxiety.*
- *Uses tactics such as mindfulness exercises and value clarifying exercises.*

Medication: When and How to Consider Pharmaceutical Support

Medication and therapy can be effective strategies for managing anxiety and other mental health issues, and they frequently work best together. Here's why.

Therapy teaches you the following skills:

A therapist can assist you in identifying the underlying causes of your anxiety, understanding your triggers, and developing coping strategies. These skills enable you to handle anxiety in the long run, even if medication is no longer required.

- *Therapy provides approaches such as Cognitive Behavioural Therapy (CBT) to address negative thought patterns.*
- *Deep breathing exercises and mindfulness meditation are examples of relaxation strategies.*
- *Communication skills enable you to convey your requirements and form healthy connections.*

Medication offers specific alleviation:

- *Anxiety drugs can provide rapid relief from debilitating symptoms, making therapy more effective.*
- *Medications can help with certain components of anxiety, such as lowering racing thoughts or boosting relaxation.*

Common anxiety drugs include:

- *Selective serotonin reuptake inhibitors (SSRIs).*
- *Serotonin-norepinephrine reuptake inhibitors (SNRIs).*
- *Benzodiazepines (short-term usage)*

The collaborative approach is key:

- **Open communication:** Establishing a trustworthy relationship with your doctor or therapist is critical. The more you tell them about your symptoms, medication experiences, and treatment goals, the better they will be able to build a strategy for your specific needs.
- **Finding the Right Fit:** There is no one-size-fits-all method. Some people feel that therapy alone is sufficient, whereas others benefit from a combination approach. Be patient; it may take some time to find the

medicine and therapy combination that best suits you.

- **Regular check-ins:** Schedule regular sessions with your doctor and therapist to check on your progress, alter medications as needed, and address any new concerns.

Here are some extra tips:

- *Do not hesitate to ask questions.*
- *Be open about any side effects you experience.*
- *Be patient and stick to your treatment strategy.*

Exploring Alternative and Complementary Therapies

While medicine and therapy are frequently used to manage anxiety, there are additional techniques that some people find beneficial. **It's important to consult with your healthcare professional before using any of these options** to ensure they are safe for you and won't interfere with any medications you're taking. Here are a few examples:

- **Acupuncture:** Acupuncture is a traditional Chinese medicinal procedure that includes putting tiny needles into certain locations of the body. Studies indicate that it may provide some alleviation from anxiety symptoms.
- **Massage Therapy:** Massage can help you relax and relieve muscle tension, which can contribute to anxiety.
- **Herbal remedies:** Some herbal medicines, like chamomile and kava, have shown the potential to alleviate anxiety symptoms. However, because herbs might mix with pharmaceuticals, it is critical to contact a healthcare practitioner before using them.

Chapter Six: Nurturing Relationships

Building Healthy Boundaries and Assertiveness Skills

Boundaries are vital for maintaining good relationships. They operate as invisible lines, defining what you will and will not tolerate. In contrast, assertive communication is the clear, straightforward, and courteous expression of your needs and desires. Here's how to master both.

1. Know Your Boundaries:

- **Identify your limitations:** Which behaviors make you feel uncomfortable or disrespected?
- **Consider your values:** What's most important to you in your relationships?
- **Be practical:** Set boundaries that are both attainable and sustainable.

2. Practice assertive communication:

- **using "I" statements:** Consider how a scenario makes you feel. For example, "I feel overwhelmed when you ask me to do last-minute favors." (Avoid using accusatory "you" sentences.)
- **Clarity and Directness:** Clearly express your wants and expectations. Avoid ambiguity.
- **Confidence, not aggression:** Maintain a relaxed and confident demeanor.

Speak clearly and maintain eye contact.

3. The Art Of Saying No:

- **It's acceptable to say no;** you don't have to justify it.
- **Offer alternatives (optional):** If applicable, suggest a different time or way to assist.

4. Respond to Boundary Violations.

- **Direct communication:** Respond calmly to the behavior and reiterate your boundaries.
- **repercussions (optional):** In some circumstances, you may need to establish repercussions for persistent boundary violations.

Here are some instances of boundary-setting and aggressive communication:

- **Scenario:** A friend keeps asking you to cancel plans at the last minute.
- **Assertive Response:** "I cherish our time together, and I feel insulted when you cancel arrangements at the last minute. In the future, if you need to postpone, please notify me as soon as possible."

Remember:

- **setting limits is not selfish:** It demonstrates self-respect and safeguards your well-being.
- **Not everyone will honor your boundaries:** It's acceptable to separate oneself from those who don't.
- **Assertiveness is a skill that requires practice:** Be patient with yourself and keep working on it.

Communication Strategies for Effective Support Networks

Here are some guidelines for communicating effectively with loved ones and support groups:

General Communication Tips:

- **Active Listening:** Pay attention to what the other person says, both orally and nonverbally. To demonstrate engagement, avoid interrupting and offer clarifying questions.
- **Empathy:** Try to understand and acknowledge their sentiments.
- **"I" statements:** Concentrate on how you feel rather than assigning blame. For example, "I feel anxious when..."
- **Clarity and directness:** Respectfully express your needs and desires. Avoid imprecise or passive-aggressive speech.

Communicating with loved ones:

- **Choose the appropriate time and place:** Make sure you have their full attention and a private area to discuss honestly.
- **Begin with appreciation:** Express gratitude for their love and support.
- **Educate them (optional):** If applicable, share facts regarding anxiety or your personal experience.
- **Concentrate on specific requests:** Rather than saying, "I need more support," specify what kind of assistance would be beneficial.
- **Be patient:** They may need some time to understand your experience.

Communicating inside Support Groups:

- **Introducing yourself (optional):** Please give your name and some information about yourself.
- **Respect others' experiences:** Everyone's journey is unique; listen without judgment.

- **Focus on sharing rather than giving advice:** Unless someone asks for it, share your own experiences and problems.
- **Be cautious of time:** Respect people's time and avoid dominating the conversation.
- **Maintain secrecy:** Respect the privacy of those who participate in the group.

Additional Tips:

- **Practice active listening skills:** There are numerous tools available online and in libraries to help you develop these skills.
- **Role-playing:** Role-playing tough discussions with a trusted friend or therapist can help boost confidence.
- **Attend a communication skills workshop:** Consider attending a workshop to improve your communication abilities.

Strategies for Resolving Conflict and Building Stronger Relationships

Conflict is unavoidable in any relationship. Disagreements arise, but how we handle them establishes the true depth of our relationships. Here are some techniques for addressing conflict constructively and building better bonds:

1. Take a step back and breathe:

- **Cool down before participating:** When emotions are strong, effective communication becomes practically impossible. Take time to calm down before tackling the problem.

2. Practice active listening:

- **Listen to comprehend rather than respond:** Give the other person your whole attention and try to see things from their perspective.
- **Acknowledge their feelings:** Validate their feelings using phrases like "I understand you're frustrated" or "It sounds like this is important to you."
- **Ask clarifying questions:** Before you answer, be sure you fully understand their point of view.

3. Communicate Assertively (Use the "I" Statements):

- **Consider how the scenario makes you feel:** Instead of accusing "you" remarks, convey your demands and worries as "I" ones.
- **Be clear and forthright:** Do not expect the other person to read your mind. Clearly express your needs and desired outcome.
- **Maintain a respectful tone:** Maintain a respectful tone, even when disagreeing.

4. Focus on Problem-Solving, Not Blame:

- **Work together to discover a solution:** Approach the situation as a team, working towards a single goal.
- **Brainstorm solutions together:** Explore multiple ideas and be willing to compromise.
- **Focus on the Future:** Do not linger on the past. The goal is to progress favorably.

5. Validate each other's feelings:

- **Recognize that both of your sentiments are valid:** Even if you disagree, it's critical to respect the other person's feelings.

6. Compromise is key:

- **Be open to compromise:** Finding a solution that benefits both parties is typically the best outcome.

- **Focus on common ground:** Look for areas of agreement and expand on them.

7. Do not be afraid to apologize:

- **Owning your mistakes:** If you've acted inappropriately, accept responsibility and sincerely apologize.
- **Consider the impact of your activities:** Explain how your behavior impacted the other individual.

8. Rebuild Trust:

- **Rebuilding trust requires time and effort:** Be patient and consistent in your actions.
- **Follow through on obligations:** Maintaining your word demonstrates your trustworthiness.

Chapter Seven: Overcoming Setbacks

Embracing Imperfection: Strategies for Letting Go of Perfectionism:

Society often bombards us with the notion that we must be flawless. Flawless grades, a picture-perfect existence on social media, a never-ending to-do list with every task completed the continuous pursuit of perfection may leave us feeling nervous, inadequate, and fatigued. What if we told you that perfection is fiction and that self-acceptance is the actual path to pleasure and well-being?

Why Perfection Is a Lie:

- **The unattainable ideal:** Perfection is a shifting target. When you attain one goal, another unreachable norm emerges.
- **The Comparison Trap:** Focusing on perfection frequently leads to comparing oneself to others, resulting in low self-esteem.
- **The stifled creativity:** Fear of making mistakes might limit our creativity and keep us from taking risks and attempting new things.

The Importance of Self-Acceptance:

- **Accepting Your Flaws:** Everyone makes mistakes and is flawed. Accepting these as part of who you are is freeing.

- **Celebrating Your qualities:** Emphasise your unique abilities and qualities. What makes you unique?
- **Developing Self-Compassion:** Treat yourself with care and understanding, as you would a friend.
- **Resilience in the Face of Failure:** Self-acceptance enables you to learn from mistakes, pick yourself up, and keep going.

Here are some tips for developing self-acceptance:

- **Challenge Negative Self-Talk:** Recognise your inner critic and replace negative ideas with affirmations that highlight your abilities and value.
- **Practice gratitude:** Concentrate on the qualities you value in yourself, your life, and the people around you.
- **Focus on Progress, not Perfection:** Celebrate your progress, no matter how tiny. Each stride forward is a step in the right direction.
- **Embrace Vulnerability:** Sharing your vulnerabilities with trusted friends and family can lead to stronger connections and a sense of belonging.
- **Forgive yourself:** Everybody makes errors. Forgive yourself, and move on.

Self-acceptance is a journey, not a destination: There will be both happy and bad days. However, by continually resisting the urge for perfection and cultivating self-compassion, you will develop a more positive self-image, increase resilience, and open the way to greater happiness and fulfilment.

Learning and Growing from Setbacks

We've all felt the sting of a squandered chance, the frustration of a failed effort. Society sometimes refers to these experiences as "failures," leaving us feeling disappointed and defeated. But what if we changed our perspectives? What if we considered failure as a stepping stone to growth and success, rather than a dead end?

The Failure Myth:

- **The "All or Nothing" Trap:** Failures should not be viewed as ultimate defeats because they provide crucial lessons.
- **dread of Trying:** The dread of failing can paralyze us, preventing us from taking risks and doing new things.
- **Missed opportunity for Growth:** Failure can bring vital insights and opportunities for learning and improvement.

The Growth Mindset:

- **Embrace the learning curve:** Every event, whether success or loss, provides an opportunity to learn and grow.
- **Develop Resilience:** The ability to recover from setbacks is critical for attaining long-term objectives.
- **Celebrate Effort:** Recognise the effort and perseverance you put in, rather than just the outcome.

Reframe Failure as a Learning Opportunity:

- **Analyzing the Situation:** What went wrong? What would you have done differently? Be honest with yourself and recognize opportunities for improvement.
- **Concentrate on Solutions:** Do not focus on the problem. Instead, come up with answers and tactics to improve your performance the next time.
- **Seek comments:** Consult with trusted mentors or coworkers for helpful comments.
- **Find Inspiration:** Consider how successful people overcame failures. Their stories can be motivating.

Here are a few suggestions to help you reframe failure:

- **Engage in positive self-talk:** Replace negative thinking like "I'm a failure" with positive comments such as "This is a learning experience" or "I'll get it next time."

- **Focus on the broad picture:** See failure as a momentary setback on your path to success.
- **Celebrate tiny wins:** Recognise your progress, no matter how modest.
- **Visualise success:** Imagine yourself accomplishing your goals. This optimistic visualization might help you gain confidence and motivation.

Embracing Risk and Uncertainty: Cultivating Resilience

If you always play it safe, life can feel rather stagnant. Sure, avoiding risks might be comforting, but it also limits your opportunities for growth and incredible experiences. The good news is that you can cultivate a growth mentality, which views obstacles and setbacks as chances to learn and progress. This, paired with taking reasonable chances, is the recipe for a rewarding and successful life!

Why Embrace Calculated Risk?

- **Unlock new opportunities:** Stepping outside of your comfort zone can lead to fascinating new opportunities, occupations, or hobbies you would not have considered otherwise.
- **Boost confidence:** Successfully handling challenges increases confidence and self-belief, allowing you to take on even greater risks in the future.
- **Boost Innovation and Creativity:** When you aren't afraid to attempt new things, you release your creativity and problem-solving abilities, resulting in innovation and breakthroughs.

How to Take Calculated Risk:

- **Start Small:** Don't do anything reckless. Begin by taking tiny, acceptable risks that will push you beyond your comfort zone but not overwhelm you.

- **Do your research:** Before taking a risk, acquire information and consider the prospective rewards and drawbacks.
- **Create a Backup Plan:** Having a safety net in place helps reduce anxiety and make you more comfortable taking the plunge.
- **Focus on the Potential Gains:** Visualise the benefits that could result from taking the risk. This might increase your motivation and excitement.

Developing a Growth Mindset:

- **Embrace challenges:** View obstacles as opportunities to learn and improve. Challenges are stepping stones, not roadblocks.
- **Celebrate Effort:** Recognise the hard effort and dedication you put in, rather than merely the outcome.
- **Learn from Mistakes:** Everybody makes mistakes. View them as useful lessons that will help you progress.
- **Embrace Feedback:** Don't be afraid of constructive criticism. Use it to find potential areas for growth.

Remember, a development mindset is a muscle that must be trained. The more you push yourself and take smart chances, the stronger and more confident you'll become.

Here are some prompts to help you get started:

- *What's the smallest risk you can take this week?*
- *Which talent have you always wanted to learn? Now is the moment to start!*
- *Have you put off an assignment or conversation? Take a deep breath, then dive in!*

Chapter Eight: Empowerment through Self-Care

The Importance of Self-Care for Women's Mental Health

Imagine yourself as a telephone. To function properly and avoid burnout, you must be charged regularly. Self-care is similar to plugging yourself in; it is a crucial activity for maintaining your physical, mental, and emotional health. When you prioritize self-care, you fill your cup, allowing you to be more present and vibrant in all aspects of your life.

Why Is Self-Care Important?

- **Reduces Stress and Anxiety:** Self-care methods such as relaxation techniques and outdoor activities can greatly lower stress and anxiety levels.
- **Boosts Energy Levels:** Making sleep, proper nutrition, and physical activity a priority helps you stay energized and ready to face daily difficulties.
- **Improves Mood and Well-Being:** Self-care helps you manage negative emotions and nurture a more cheerful mindset.
- **Improves Focus and Concentration:** When you're well-rested and taking care of yourself, you'll be able to focus better and work more efficiently.
- **Strengthens Relationships:** By caring for yourself, you have more emotional bandwidth to connect with and support the people in your life.

Identify Your Self-Care Needs:

- **Each person's self-care needs are unique:** What works for one person may not work for another. Here are some guidelines for determining your self-care needs:
- **Listen to Your Body:** Be aware of physical indications such as weariness, headaches, and muscle strain. These could indicate that you need to prioritize rest, relaxation, or movement.
- **Evaluate Your Emotions:** Do you feel stressed, anxious, or overwhelmed? Determine what activities will assist you handle these feelings.
- **Consider your values:** What is most important to you in life? Plan self-care activities that are consistent with your values.
- **Experiment and Reflect:** Try different self-care techniques to find what makes you feel good. Consider what works and doesn't.

Below are some examples of self-care habits to consider:

- **Physical Self-Care:** Physical self-care includes getting adequate sleep, eating healthy meals, exercising frequently, using relaxation techniques (deep breathing, meditation), and spending time outdoors.
- **Mental Self-Care:** Setting boundaries, practicing gratitude, journaling, spending time with loved ones, and participating in enjoyable hobbies are all examples of mental self-care.
- **Emotional Self-Care:** Emotional self-care entails healthily expressing your feelings, making time for quiet thought, and unplugging from technology.

Creating Personalized Self-Care Plans

Self-care is not a one-size-fits-all solution. What calms your dearest buddy may make you feel restless. The key to good self-care is developing a personalized strategy that addresses your requirements and preferences. Here is how to start:

1. Listen to Your Body, Mind, and Soul:

- **Body Awareness:** Pay attention to physical indicators indicating tension or tiredness. Have a strong desire to sleep? Feeling achy? These could be indicators that your body requires rest, relaxation techniques, or movement.
- **Emotional Check-In:** How do you feel overall? Stressed? Anxious? Identifying your emotions allows you to select self-care activities that target them.
- **Values Check:** What is most important to you in life? Consider engaging in activities that are consistent with your ideals.

2. Encourage Self-Discovery through Experimentation:

- **Explore Various Activities:** There's a huge variety of self-care methods! Try meditation, yoga, journaling, spending time with loved ones, or engaging in hobbies that you enjoy.
- **Pay Attention to Your Feelings:** Consider how each activity impacts you. Does it make you feel energized, relaxed, or centered?
- **Refine and repeat:** Create a self-care toolkit based on your experiences, including activities that will help you feel your best.

3. Develop a Self-Care Plan:

- **Schedule Self-Care Time:** Treat self-care as you would any other crucial appointment. Set aside time in your calendar for things that nourish you, even if it's only 15 minutes per day.

- **Variety is key:** Include a variety of self-care techniques in your plan to meet different needs throughout the week.
- **Start Small and Build Gradually:** Don't overwhelm yourself. Begin with short, doable self-care routines, gradually increasing the duration and frequency as you develop a pattern.

Here are some more recommendations for developing your personalized self-care plan:

- **Create a self-care toolkit:** List your favorite self-care activities, relaxing techniques, and motivational quotes. Keep this toolkit on hand for when you need a little extra self-care.
- **Find an accountability partner:** Share your self-care strategy with a friend or family member, and ask them to keep you responsible. Knowing that someone is checking in might keep you on track.
- **Make it Fun and Engaging:** Self-care should be pleasant! Choose hobbies that you enjoy doing.
- **Be adaptable:** Life gets busy, and your self-care needs may shift. Be adaptable and change your plan as needed.

Radical Self-Love: Embracing Your Authentic Self

In a world that frequently demands uniformity, recognizing your distinct identity and practicing self-acceptance is a revolutionary act. It's about letting go of the need to fit in and embracing your true self. Here's why self-acceptance is essential for realizing your full potential and living a bright life:

Why should you embrace your uniqueness?

- **You Are One-of-a-Kind:** Your idiosyncrasies, hobbies, and experiences form a magnificent tapestry that is entirely yours. Embrace what makes you unique!
- **The world needs your light:** Your unique perspective and talents enrich and diversify the planet. Don't turn down the light!
- **Authenticity is magnetic:** People gravitate towards genuine interactions. When you accept your authentic self, you attract individuals who value who you are.

The Power of Self-Acceptance:

- **Inner Peace and Confidence:** Self-acceptance frees you from the need for external validation, fostering a profound sense of inner peace and confidence.
- **Resilience in the Face of Challenges:** When you embrace yourself, flaws, and all, you're better able to deal with criticism and recover from setbacks.
- **Openness to Growth:** Self-acceptance does not imply settling. It helps you to grow and learn while preserving your distinct essence.

Tips for Celebrating Your Uniqueness and Practicing Self-Acceptance:

- **Challenge Negative Self-Talk:** Recognise and replace negative thoughts about yourself with affirmations that highlight your strengths and values.
- **Find Your Tribe:** Surround yourself with individuals who value and celebrate your characteristics.
- **Celebrate Your Achievements:** Recognise your accomplishments, big or small, and be proud of who you are becoming.
- **Focus on Your Passions:** Engage in things that spark your interest and bring you delight.
- **Practice Gratitude:** Recognise the qualities you admire about yourself, your life, and the people around you.

Conclusion

Managing anxiety is a journey rather than a destination. It requires focus and work, and it can feel like you're taking two steps forward and one back. But here's the thing: even modest strides forward are achievements to celebrate! Take a minute to acknowledge your progress; you deserve a pat on the back.

Why should you acknowledge your progress?

- **Motivation Booster:** Recognising your victories, no matter how big or small, keeps you motivated to keep going.
- **Increased confidence:** Seeing your success gives you confidence in your capacity to control worry properly.
- **Shifting your focus:** Recognising your accomplishments helps you move your focus away from obstacles and towards the positive progress you're making.

How to Celebrate your Victories:

- **Track your progress:** Keep a notebook or make a list to record your accomplishments, no matter how tiny.
- **Reward yourself:** After accomplishing a milestone, reward yourself with something you appreciate.
- **Share Your Wins:** Celebrate your accomplishments beside a supportive friend or family member.

- **Take a moment to reflect:** Take time to acknowledge your talents and coping methods after dealing with a difficult scenario successfully.

Here are some examples of progress worth celebrating:

- *Trying out a new coping mechanism for the first time.*
- *Leaving the house while feeling nervous.*
- *Talking about your anxiety with a loved one.*
- *Recognizing your anxiety triggers and remaining cool.*
- *Having less or less severe anxiety symptoms.*

Maintaining Positive Changes for a Calmer, More Confident You

Congratulations! You've started on a path to a calmer, more confident existence, and you're making positive adjustments. That is wonderful! However, remaining on track is not always easy. Here are some suggestions to help you retain those great changes and keep going forward:

Solidify Your Foundation:

- **Identify your "Why":** Remember why you began this adventure in the first place. What do you hope to achieve? Keeping your goals clear will help you stay motivated.
- **Celebrate Milestones:** Recognise your accomplishments, big or small. This promotes healthy behaviors and helps you move forward. (See previous suggestion for celebrating victory!)
- **Practice self-compassion:** Change requires time and effort. When you make mistakes, be fair to yourself. Everyone makes mistakes, so get back on track!

Develop Sustainable Habits:

- **Focus on Small, Consistent Steps:** Making major adjustments can be overwhelming. Begin with simple, attainable goals and progressively build on them.

- **Integrate Self-Care:** Give priority to activities that nourish your mind, body, and spirit. A well-rested, relaxed self is better able to face obstacles and retain beneficial changes.
- **Find an Accountability Partner:** Discuss your goals with a supportive friend or family member who can motivate and hold you accountable.

Accept the inevitable setbacks:

- **Consider Setbacks as Learning Opportunities:** Everyone faces setbacks. View them as opportunities to learn, change your strategy, and become even stronger.
- **Practice Resilience:** Improve your ability to recover from setbacks. Do not allow failures to hinder your development.
- **Concentrate on what you can control:** Life throws curveballs. Concentrate on the areas you can control, such as your attitude, reactions, and dedication to your goals.

Here are some more tips:

- **Seek Help:** If you need help managing anxiety or keeping beneficial changes, don't be afraid to seek professional assistance.
- **Find inspiration:** Read books, listen to podcasts, or watch documentaries about self-improvement and anxiety management. Surround yourself with favorable influences.
- **Visualise Success:** Spend a few minutes each day visualizing yourself attaining your goals. This optimistic visualization might help you gain confidence and motivation.